ALL KINDS OF FAMILIES

FAMILIES THROUGH
DIVORCE

SLOANE HUGHES

PowerKiDS
press.

New York

Published in 2021 by The Rosen Publishing Group, Inc.
29 East 21st Street, New York, NY 10010

First Edition

Editor: Michelle Denton
Book Design: Reann Nye

Photo Credits: Cover LightField Studios/Shutterstock.com; Series Art Vladislav Noseek/Shutterstock.com; p. 5 Rido/Shutterstock.com; p. 7 miodrag ignjatovic/E+/getty Images; p. 9 bbernard/Shutterstock.com; p. 11 Yagi Studio/DigitalVision/Getty Images; p. 13 PeopleImages/E+/Getty Images; p. 15 Westend61/Getty Images; p. 17 ©iStockphoto.com/fizkes; p. 19 Thomas Barwick/DigitalVision/Getty Images; p. 21 FG Trade/E+/Getty Images.

Some of the images in this book illustrate individuals who are models. The depictions do not imply actual situations or events.

Library of Congress Cataloging-in-Publication Data

Names: Hughes, Sloane, author.
Title: Families through divorce / Sloane Hughes.
Description: New York : PowerKids Press, [2021] | Series: All kinds of
   families | Includes index.
Identifiers: LCCN 2019045960 | ISBN 9781725317734 (paperback) | ISBN
   9781725317758 (library binding) | ISBN 9781725317741 (6 pack)
Subjects: LCSH: Divorced parents–Juvenile literature. | Divorce–Juvenile
   literature. | Families–Juvenile literature.
Classification: LCC HQ759.915 .H84 2020 | DDC 306.89–dc23
LC record available at https://lccn.loc.gov/2019045960

Manufactured in the United States of America

CPSIA Compliance Information: Batch #CSPK20. For Further Information contact Rosen Publishing, New York, New York at 1-800-237-9932.

Find us on

ALL KINDS OF FAMILIES

FAMILIES THROUGH
DIVORCE

SLOANE HUGHES

CONTENTS

MANY KINDS OF FAMILIES

When you think about a family, the picture that comes to mind might include a mother, a father, and children. But families can look very different from one another!

There are many reasons parents get divorced, or **legally** undo their marriage. Sometimes they don't get along, sometimes they want different things in life, and sometimes they've grown apart. About one-third of the marriages in the United States end in divorce. If your parents are getting a divorce, you're not alone.

Even if parents get divorced, it doesn't mean they love their children any less.

DIVORCE VS. SEPARATION

Divorce is what happens when two people who are married decide they don't want to be married anymore. After a divorce, the two people are independent from one another. All their **assets** are **split** between them.

Other times, people choose to be legally separated but not divorced. In a separation, the two people remain married, but they live in different homes. People choose legal separation over divorce for many reasons. For example, they might wish to file their taxes together or to keep their family's health-care plan the same.

Parents who divorce make many legal decisions that will affect the whole family for many years.

WHAT IS CUSTODY?

After a divorce, a court may decide who has custody, or the legal right to take care of the children. It can be one or both of the parents, but sometimes it's someone else, such as a grandparent.

Physical custody means a parent has the right to have their children live with them. Even if one parent isn't living with their children, they might still have a joint legal custody agreement. That means the parents must make decisions about their children together.

Sometimes, only one parent has custody
of their children. These families may

AFTER A DIVORCE

There are many decisions parents must make after a divorce. One or both parents may find new homes. Sometimes the children stay in one place and the parents move in and out. Other times, children travel back and forth between their parents' homes.

Parents may have to work out a visitation **schedule** of when each of them can see the children. If a court decides it's unsafe for a child to be alone with one parent, they may grant that person **supervised visitation** or take away their visitation rights completely.

Sometimes children spend half their time with one parent and half their time with the other.

11

A NEW NORMAL

After a divorce, many things might look different. It might feel very messy as everyone tries to get used to their new normal. For kids who split their time between two homes, it can feel very **frustrating** to have to uproot their lives for a weekend, a week, or even longer at a time.

However, with time, things will start to feel more normal again. After all, children of divorced parents are still part of a family. Divorce doesn't change how much parents love their kids.

For some children, both parts of their family may live near each other. For others, they can be far apart!

13

LOTS OF EMOTIONS

It's normal to have a lot of feelings about divorce, even feelings that don't often go together. For example, someone may feel **relief** if their parents were fighting a lot and they get along better when living apart. At the same time, they might feel nervous about having two different homes.

It's OK to have both these feelings and more. Still, it's important to show respect to everyone. Sometimes it's helpful to remember that everyone else is going through a big change too.

It's good to talk about your feelings about a divorce, even if you're not completely sure what to say. Perhaps start by saying, "I feel upset, but I don't know why."

15

TALKING IT OUT

Children of divorced parents may be angry with one or both of their parents. That's OK. However, it's important not to let emotions have too much control over the way you act. Acting out is not a good **coping** method.

If you're having a hard time dealing with your feelings, try putting them into words. If it's hard to speak about them, maybe try writing a letter. If these methods don't work, try talking to an adult you trust, such as another family member or a **guidance counselor**.

Think about what you want from a talk about emotions. Do you want to be heard and understood? Are you looking for some kind of advice?

17

SIMILAR AND DIFFERENT

Many things might be different after a divorce. If your family has gone through a divorce, you may see one or both of your parents less often, or you may have a new home. You may be starting at a new school. All these changes can be scary, but they can also sometimes be fun. Maybe you'll make new friends. Maybe there's a nice ice cream shop in your new neighborhood. A lot of things might be the same too. You can still enjoy spending time with each parent.

Cell phones have made it easier to stay in touch. Many children use video chat to speak to one parent while they're visiting the other.

19

NEW RELATIONSHIPS

After things calm down, it's possible that one parent or both might start a new relationship. If this happens in your family, it can be hard to accept that a divorced parent has moved on, but it shouldn't change the bond you have with your parent. No matter what, your parent should want what's best for you.

In this case, try to spend some time with the new adult in your life. You don't have to force a relationship with them, but you do have to show them respect.

Creating a relationship with someone new doesn't mean you've **replaced** your other parent—it means you're adding another person into your life!

21

ALWAYS A FAMILY

If you or someone you know is having issues getting used to a divorce, it's important to talk to someone about it. If you have a concern, let your parents or another trusted adult know about it. Perhaps you can solve the problem together. If you know someone whose parents are getting divorced, offer support! Even just being there to listen can be helpful.

Getting used to the changes after a divorce can be hard, but divorced families are still families. They can offer the same love and support they did before.

GLOSSARY

asset: An item of property or something someone owns.

cope: To deal with and try to find help for problems.

frustrating: Causing feelings of anger and annoyance.

guidance counselor: A person who gives help and advice to students, often in school.

legally: Allowed by law or rules.

relief: A good feeling that occurs when something unpleasant or distressing stops or does not happen.

replace: To take the place of.

schedule: To plan for a certain time, or a list of times when certain things will happen.

supervised visitation: When a parent is allowed to see their child in a safe and watched setting.

split: To divide into portions, parts, or fragments.

INDEX

WEBSITES

Due to the changing nature of Internet links, PowerKids Press has developed an online list of websites related to the subject of this book. This site is updated regularly. Please use this link to access the list: www.powerkidslinks.com/akof/divorce